Weather Wise

Snow

Helen Cox Cannons

Heinemann
LIBRARY

Chicago, Illinois

© 2015 Heinemann Library
an imprint of Capstone Global Library, LLC
Chicago, Illinois

Edited by Siân Smith and John-Paul Wilkins
Designed by Philippa Jenkins and Peggie Carley
Picture research by Ruth Blair
Production by Victoria Fitzgerald
Originated by Capstone Global Library Ltd
Printed in the United States of America in
North Mankato, MN. 052017 010519RP

Library of Congress Cataloging in Publication Data
Cataloging-in-publication information is on file with the Library of Congress.
ISBN 978-1-4846-0546-2 (hardcover)
ISBN 978-1-4846-0556-1 (paperback)
ISBN 978-1-4846-0571-4 (eBook PDF)

Photo Credits
Dreamstime: Mira Janacek, 7; Getty Images: Kristian Sekulic/E+, cover; iStockphoto: Dreef, 8, 23 (top), ParkerDeen, 9, simplytheyu, 22; Shutterstock: Gajus, 17, 23 (bottom), Kostenko Maxim, 5, KSLight, 20, Olga Miltsova, 11, oliveromg, 21, Pavel Svoboda, 19, Sunny Forest, 4, urciser, 6, vikiri, 10, Waj, 18

We would like to thank John Horel for his invaluable help in the preparation of this book.

Every effort has been made to contact copyright holders of material reproduced in this book. Any omissions will be rectified in subsequent printings if notice is given to the publisher.

Contents

What Is Snow?

Snow is pieces of frozen water that fall from the sky.

These pieces of frozen water can form **snowflakes**.

Types of Snow

Snowflakes fall when it is cold. When wet snowflakes stick together, heavy snow falls.

When it is very cold, the snowflakes do not stick together. This is called light snow.

Heavy snowfall with strong winds is called a **blizzard**.

Blizzards make it hard to be outside.

Is Snow White?

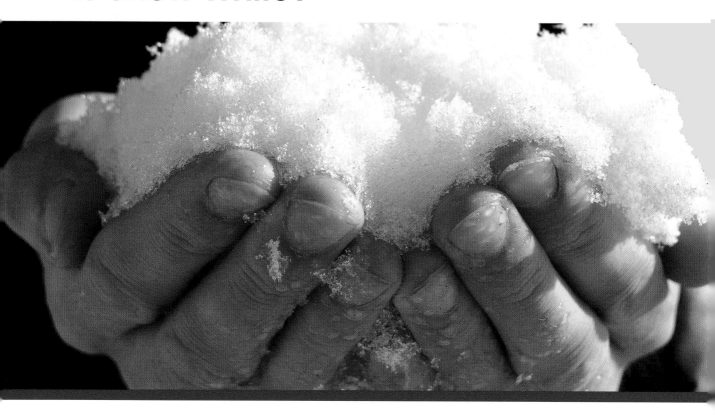

Snow looks white, but it is not.
Snow is clear.

Snow looks white because of the light from the Sun. On a sunny day, snow is very bright to look at.

How Does Snow Form?

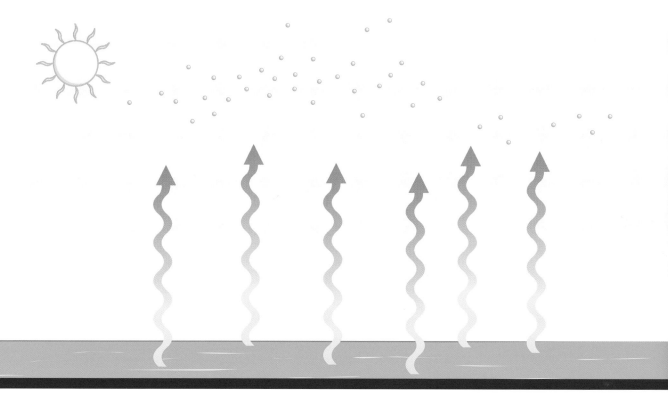

When the Sun warms water, some of it becomes a gas called **vapor**.

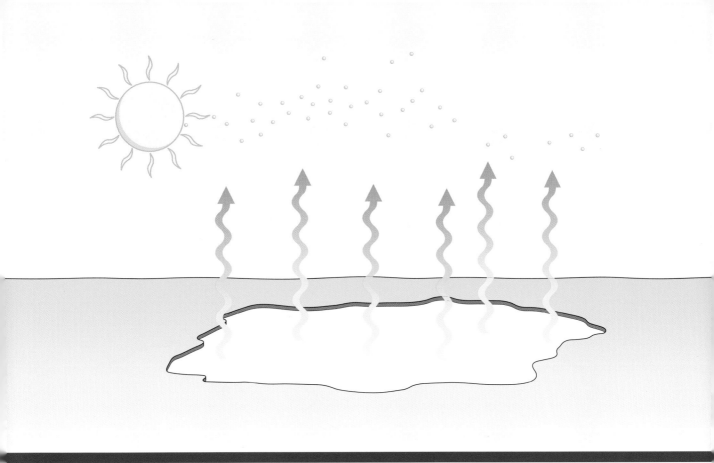

Water vapor comes from **oceans** and lakes.

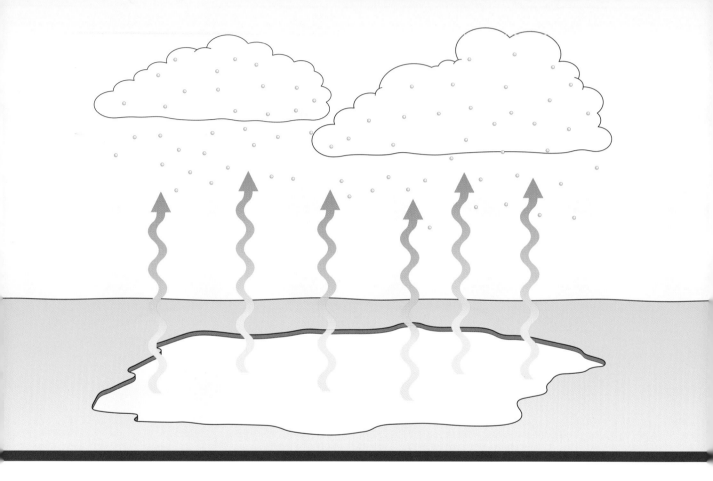

The water vapor rises into the air. Then it cools down and turns into tiny drops of water. The tiny drops make clouds.

frozen water vapor

If it is very cold, water vapor freezes in the clouds.

The frozen water drops join together to make snowflakes. When snowflakes

get too heavy, they fall to the ground.

snowflake

Some snowflakes melt before they reach the ground. Others stay frozen because the air is so cold.

Snow Around the World

Some places that have hot weather
never get snow.

Some places that have cold weather
get snow most of the time.

How Does Snow Help Us?

 Snow brings water back to Earth.
Plants need water to grow.

Snow can be fun!

Did You Know?

All snowflakes are different from each other. Snowflakes come in many different patterns.

Picture Glossary

 **blizzard** period of heavy snowfall with strong winds

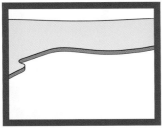 **ocean** large body of water

 **snowflake** piece of frozen water that has fallen from the sky

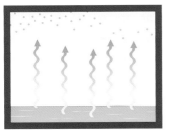 **vapor** gas created by heating water

Index

Notes for Parents and Teachers

Before Reading
Assess background knowledge. Ask: What is snow? How does snow form? How does snow help us?

After Reading
Recall and reflection: Ask children how snowflakes are formed. What facts about snow surprised them?

Sentence knowledge: Ask children to look at page 6. How many sentences are on this page? How can they tell?

Word recognition: Have children point at the word *cold* on page 7. Can they find *cold* on page 19? Have children point to things in this book that are cold.